LAUGH

Dikachi Mann

Author contact;

Author page: http://www.amazon.com/Dikachi-Mann/e/B015G6U6BU

Facebook page:
https://www.facebook.com/DikachiMann/

Preface

Life often will throw us curveballs when we least expect. Many a time these moments derail us from our normal routines and perspectives on what life is all about, but that should not be the case. Indeed there is a silver lining beyond every storm and if we can only make it through, we will realize we usually do not have the full picture of every situation.

Over several months of my life, after I had almost given up on life, I carefully documented what would otherwise be the deepest life changing lessons I learnt going through those uncertain times. Twenty-eight of those lessons are carefully distilled in this book as quotes. On the surface, these quotes are helpful and applicable to daily life, however, if you read just one a day and spend time mulling over it through the day, you will discover it unveils an answer to the power of laughter. An answer that lay before your eyes, but you never could comprehend or see before! How? The human mind works in such a way that once it is rightly focused it can solve any problem it sets to resolve.

This book gives you that focus which you require.

As you read these quotes, I believe these words will not just be the light to help you on your daily life's path, but also a ready companion in times of despair. Finally, I encourage you at the end of this book to come up with a personal declaration, which should become your own personal mantra to laugh by every day.

I bid you god-speed as you begin your transformational journey to a life filled with laughter!

Acknowledgements

I am thankful for the life circumstances that brought me to the point of writing this book. I also owe thanks to the individuals who have taken part in my life's story so far, most especially my family, loved ones and friends, who made the journey bearable.

I would not be who I am today without you.

Thank you!

Dikachi Mann,
19th March 2019.

Why should you laugh?......

A good laugh is medicine for the soul

Laughter is life's music.

Like the sun defines day….

Laughter defines life!

Laughter does not always emanate from a joyful heart. Sometimes, when you don't feel like it….LAUGH, it helps to push the pain away.

Learn from little children….how easily they laugh!

Laughter neither thrives nor has a place in a gathering of mourning and sorrow.

There is no intimacy without laughter in its midst.

Do not be fazed when people laugh at you, for their laughter often ensues from ignorance, when one is unaware of your life's process.

When you laugh, let it be genuine!

Otherwise, please do not laugh.

Loud and unruly laughter only makes one out as a fool.

Joy and Laughter are often not limited by circumstances or happenings around you, but a certainty in what lies within you.

Laugh as often as you can. It is GOOD medicine for your body, mind and soul.

Laughter has it's time and place.

The possibility of doing the seemingly impossible is quite often preceded by a subtle, yet hope-filled laugh.

There is no folly worse than the laughter of a deceitful friend.

There is power in your laughter.

Let your laughter rewrite the sad stories of people's lives.

Offer it up willingly!

Good humor and laughter uplift the heaviest of hearts and brighten the darkest of faces.

Crying hard and laughing hard, both help to unclutter the soul.

Laughter without hope is meaningless.

The most unplanned of occurrences often leave a smile on our faces and laughter in our hearts.

Great is the joy of he who finds satisfaction and laughter in the little things of life.

Unplanned, chaotic laughter often leaves people wondering if you are insane.

Laugh nonetheless!

Use your laughter wisely.

Not every tool is used on all occasions.

Take as many moments in your day as you can to find your laughter. It's worth it.

Laughter inspired by the company of a spouse or loved one banishes the fear of an uncertain future.

Keep those who cause you to laugh close! They are the people you need in your most trying times, to help clear the darkness.

The true sound of a content and grateful heart is laughter.

***A** house full of laughter is a house full of love and trust.*

Laughter by its very nature is contagious,
and if you keep laughing long enough,
everyone around you would too.

Now, that's something worth spreading!

Laughter is often like a wave or strong wind.

You don't fight against it.

You ride it.

My Declaration

I *refuse to allow my life's circumstances to determine my state of mind and choices. Though my road may not be as easy as I had hoped, I still choose to celebrate my journey thus far. So today I choose to laugh! I vow to do my best always, to laugh at myself when I fall, and to rise up once again….and try!*

For life is too short, to be dead serious always.

I vow to infuse my day with the colours of my laughter, making someone else's day a little bit brighter as I make mine. For in so doing, I would have shone my light in the midst of so much darkness and inspired more lights to shine.

This will make my world a better place and my existence much more fulfilling!

My name is Dikachi Mann and I choose tc #LAUGH

Your Declaration

My name

is…………………………………..

and I choose tc #LAUGH

About the author

Dikachi Mann is in his thirties, an avid reader, a lover of life and all things beautiful. He currently works managing people. He loves to speak at events and travel the world.

He currently lives in Scotland and this is the concluding book of his 3-part book series; LIVE, LOVE and LAUGH. He is currently writing his first antonym which is a collection of short stories and poems.

www.ingramcontent.com/pod-product-compliance
Ingram Content Group UK Ltd.
Pitfield, Milton Keynes, MK11 3LW, UK
UKHW042001190726
13854UKWH00005B/2108

9 781544 931593